KHICHDI:
Simple, Soulful & Soothing

By

CauldronSisterss

Title   : **KHICHDI: Simple, Soulful & Soothing**
Author : **Ratika Bhargava & Riccha Khetan**
Copyright © **Ratika Bhargava & Riccha Khetan** 2021
All rights reserved

First published in 2021
First Edition 2021

Table of Contents

*In loving memory of our **Bauji Shri Govind Ram ji Khetan**.*

*For our **Mom, Dad, Father-in-law** (Ratika's) & **Rahul** who have
been the main inspiration for our cooking!*

Tanay*(our baby boo) for bearing with us
when we were away for research!*

Introduction

Khichdi.

Wherever in India we are from, put a bowl of this dal and rice combination in front of us and we will have a name for it - Khichdi, Khichuri, Pongal, Khichda or even Bisi Bele Bhaat!

So, what exactly is Khichdi?

In India, the term Khichdi, when used broadly, implies a mishmash, mixture, or hodgepodge. That said, inmy opinion, none of those words do justice to explain Khichdi. At its simplest, Khichdi is a one-pot complete meal. But to Indians it is an emotion. It is an undemanding dish, requiring simple and easily accessed ingredients, minimal skill and time to cook. Khichdi embodies all that warm mushy-ness that we crave in comfort food – like a warm hug in a bowl. But this simplicity of texture, allows one to personalize one's bowl to one's taste. Wherever in India we are from, chances are we will identify with a favorite variation!

Like so many aspects of Indian cuisine, Khichdi is as universal as it is diverse. A quintessential comfort food, it is simple to make, and yet so easy to customize depending on where one is, what is available and who or what occasion the khichdi is being made for. At their simplest, Khichdis call for rice and dal, staple ingredients easily available in most Indian homes but each of these offers endless varioatins. Rice is preferred but other grains like millets may be swapped for it. When it comes to the dal part, moong is favoured, but most pulses work, and combinations of various pulses can make things even more interesting! A third variable comes in the form of spices, which make the possibilities endless! I am not even getting into variations that can be made using embellishments of vegetables and meat. But then when it comes to the table, everyone has a specific combination they love most no?

***

That we have myriad versions and individual preferences for Khichdi should come as no surprise. As an agrarian country, Khichdi has long been a part of our culinary repertoire. I visualise the history of Khichdi as intertwined with the birth and evolution of Indian cuisine, going back to prehistoric times, when hunter-gatherer communities foraged for grains and cooked them all together by boiling in a pot.

Khichdi has been mentioned time and again in historical medical texts, folklore, common expression and accounts of rulers, travelers and invaders of Hindustan, suggesting that this dish or its variants have been long consumed in what we know today as India. The Moroccan traveler Ibn Battuta came across "Kishri", a dish in India, comprised of rice and mung beans, around the year 1350. "Khichri" also finds mention in accounts by Russian adventurer Afanasiy Nikitin, who travelled to the Indian subcontinent in the 15th century. It was very popular with the Mughals, including Humayun, Akbar and Jehangir. Ain-i-Akbari, a 16th-century document written by Mughal Emperor Akbar's vizier, Abu'l-Fazl ibn Mubarak, mentions the recipe for 'Khichri' in seven variations!

The other aspect that shows how intrinsically connected Khichdi is to our roots is the fact that it is part of so many social occasions. In fact in popular idiom, khichdi is often used to describe circumstances that become a mess! But more seriously, from birth to mourning ceremonies, in sickness, health and festivity, Khichdi is omnipresent on the menu. And with our agrarian background, Khichdi is part of our festivals too - especially harvest festivals. The festival of Makar Sankranti which is celebrated in many avatars across India gives Khichdi great prominence. So much so that most regions that celebrate Sankranti will do so with a local version of the Khichdi. Which is why the festival is also referred to as Khichdi Sankrant in many parts of the country!

***

A dish that embedded itself so deeply in the ethos of a cuisine and survived millennia did not do so on the basis of taste alone. There's also the health perspective. Khichdi has its origins in Ayurveda. According to Ayurveda, Khichdi is a dish that can be eaten year-round with variations made to adjust to the diet. It is light on the gut, yet it gives you energy and satiety. From infants (as one of their earliest solid foods), to people of all ages Khichdi is the first thing many doctors or elders in the family recommend when you are ill. This is why Khichdi is also part of the regular offerings of everyday meals in homes across India, not to mention a preferred food for the young, infirm, ill and elderly or anyone with a weak digestion. What we don't appreciate enough is just what makes Khichdi so wholesome, because it is not apparent.

Our Indian dal-rice meals or Khichdis are combinations of cereal and pulse that offer the human body a complete nutritive profile. In isolation, cereals and pulses have incomplete amino acid profiles, but when eaten in combination they complement each other nutritionally and the amino acid profile is complete. And then there are all the other elements, the spices that assist the body in assimilating the bio-nutritive properties of ingredients along with adding their functional properties to the mix. So you get all the proteins and carbohydrates along with micronutrients in one delicious bowl! All of these health benefits make khichdi a universal panacea. The fact that a khichdi can be customized to treat vagaries of season, and individual illness also stands in its favour. For example, Khichdi may be tweaked to have more asafetida to aid an upset stomach or digestion, it can be spiked with pepper to warm the body on cold, rainy days.

***

Which often makes me ask, can there be a more Indian dish than Khichdi?

Khichdi is quintessentially Indian! No other cuisine cooks a combination of cereal and pulse quite like this because no other cuisine in the world uses plant based foods, specifically the cereal-pulse combination, as uniquely and to the degree we do in Indian cuisine. There is no other dish with a similar degree of pervasiveness and variation. It cuts across all barriers of income, religion, caste and creed. Every regional and community cuisine has its signature version with both vegetarian and non-vegetarian versions that incorporate fish, fowl and meat. Khichdi can be simple or made festive. And this book offers a beautiful tribute to this humble dish. It has been a privilege to be associated with the making of it. I have watched how passionately Ratika and Riccha have worked to bring out some truly beautiful recipes from the lengths and breadths of India and I, for one, cannot wait to start cooking from it!

Rushina Munshaw-Ghildiyal
Author / Culinary Consultant / Culinary Chronicler
Founder & Owner - A Perfect Bite Consulting & APB Cook Studio

Acknowledgements

We are so proud to present '**KHICHDI: Simple, Soulful & Soothing**' to interested readers and culinary enthusiasts around the globe. However, the celebration is incomplete without expressing our gratitude to those who have supported us in this journey. We thank our mentors whose guidance helped us hone and refine our skills. This book would not have been possible without the blessings of our Guru, mentor **Mr. Sandeep Sethi**. We are also thankful to **Ms. Rita Taneja** & **SV Public School**. A big shout out to all our family members, friends, clients, and staff – You have been our rock solid support throughout our journey.

As you turn the pages of this book, you will find endearing memories and mouthwatering recipes by star contributors. We know you will be pleasantly surprised at how easy these recipes are and you will make them again for sure!

We would like to thank our Star contributors:

Ms. Raageshwari
Chef Vicky Ratnani
Mr. Atul Sikand
Chef Anahita Dhondy
Chef Saby Gorai
Chef Jyoti Vishnani
Chef Izzat Hussain
Chef Altamsh Patel
Chef Ashish Bhasin
Mr. Kalyan Karmarkar
Ms. Saee Koranne Khandekar
Mr. Tikku
Ms. Shubra Chatterji
Mr Nitin Hajela
Mrs. Madhushree & Mr. Anindya Sundar Basu

We would like to specially thank **Ms. Rushina Munshaw-Ghildiyal** for mentoring us through this book project and the beautiful introduction.

We would also like to thank, from the bottom of our hearts, our sponsors

Pindproduce
Bhagat Mishthan Bhandar
Saccha Moti Sabudana
Fit Body & Soul

Book edited by
Bhavana Bhat

Riccha Khetan   Ratika Bhargava

Authors' Note

Ever since we started cooking, each recipe in our diary, every whiff in our cauldron, all the textures of prepared dishes, and the entire experience of putting together a meal has been incredibly satisfying. Our fascination with food started when we were kids. We'd watch our parents cook together for special family dinners over weekends and festivals. So cooking and experimenting came naturally to both of us without having to attend culinary school.

In 2015, with a generous dollop of faith in ourselves, we decided to embark on the ambitious journey that is CauldronSisterss. Our mission is to treat the city of Jaipur to our culinary zest. We, the CauldronSisterss deliver 'home-cooked, restaurant- style food' to family gatherings, corporate meetings, high-end lifestyle exhibitions and pretty much everywhere there's a party. Our masalas and pickles will remind you of home wherever you are in the world!

Most Indians have their personal favourite version of Khichdi along with memories and stories to share about it. As a tribute, in 2018, we released our first-ever book **'India ki Khichdi**' which had 51 Khichdi recipes. And that was just the beginning! It set off a passionate affair with Khichdi for us. After 3 years of diligent research and hands-on experience, we are thrilled to reintroduce India ki Khichdi as **'Khichdi: Simple, Soulful, Soothing'**.With this book, we hope to put the spotlight back on what we think is an ancient superfood of India.

In the process of writing this book, we have discovered new cultures, secrets of Indian cooking and its history. So dear reader, look forward to a delicious journey of exploring Khichdi and the stories behind its myriad versions in this book. We have been researching, trialing and taste-testing the recipes in this book to capture the vivid tastes of locally made Khichdis as closely as we could. Having said that, we would like to mention that while some of the recipes hit the spot with local flavours, others will have the signature Cauldronsisterss' tadka!

As we add this little book to our plethora of offerings, we cannot help marvel at how far we have come from those early experimenting days in the kitchen! We are really excited to bring you this, our latest offering, Khichdi and all that it means to us!

We are proud to say that all the proceeds from the sale of our book 'Khichdi: Simple, Soulful, Soothing' will be donated to social causes that are close to our hearts like welfare of girl children, senior citizen and animal welfare organisations.

Love,

Ratika & Riccha

<u>Disclaimer: This book is not intended to provide any medical advice or treatment to readers.</u>

Our Memories With Khichdi

In November 2017 Khichdi was recognized as the 'Brand India' food. That caught our attention. We realised that India is home to diverse cultures, ethnicities and religions, and has a distinct food palette. And while it can be difficult to pin down a single dish that represents the country, khichdi comes pretty close! It has infinite variations with personalised favourites. It is relished by everyone, regardless of caste, class, economic stature and income. And it is so SO MUCH MORE than 'food for sick people!'

For a typical Marwari, food is truly satisfying only when everything is poured onto a plate, rather than being separated into various katoris or bowls. In our home we like to pair khichdi with Kadhi, like the Gujaratis do. And freshly churned white butter is always the ideal accompaniment to khichdi in our family.

In fact as we wrote, we fondly remembered how our grandfather, a staunch Marwari, would ladle Bajra khichdi onto his steel thaali, top it with white butter, mash it up with his index & ring finger till the khichdi changed colour to white-ish and then relish it. He made eating food look like art!

Our tryst with the humble Khichdi started then, as children. Our mother would spoon generous dollops of home-made white butter onto servings for the then skinny Ritzzy in the hope that she would gain some much needed weight. In fact, Ritzzy (Riccha), still recalls the flavour of that '*bachpan ki moong dal khichdi*' and *Ma ka pyaar*! Ratzz (Ratika) on the other hand, didn't develop an affinity for the regular rice based khichdi but loves the Bajra khichdi which is a Rajasthani winter staple with a passion!

And this love for khichdi has passed down through the generations! Ratzz's son Tanay has developed a liking for khichdi since he was little. We have never fed him packaged food. He was always fed varieties of khichdi, sometimes with mashed vegetables, arhar dal, sometimes with matar. Even today, his favourite food is a simple khichdi. Which means that when Ratzz is in a hurry or simply confused about what to make for dinner, a quick masaledar khichdi is something the family always enjoys.

Four generations of our family have loved and relished Khichdi together. And we hope this book, with its many varieties of recipes, will add to your family memories of Khichdi too!

Quick Tips from The CauldronSisterss
for Easy Cooking

1. Always soak dal, rice, and grains for a minimum of half an hour before you start cooking.

2. Khichdi is an overcooked dish, so it's okay to give it an extra whistle in the pressure cooker

3. Every region has its own climate and water quality which could affect the cooking process. Feel free to adjust the given cooking time until the dish is properly cooked. You can also tweak the amount of water you add based on your preference.

4. Follow the recipe but get creative and use your instincts for preference of vegetables, spice level, etc.

5. Traditionally, Indian khichdi is served with four accompaniments - curds or yoghurt, ghee or clarified butter, achaar or pickle and papad or fried crisps. We've included region specific accompaniments for a more authentic experience.

6. Unless you are in a tearing hurry, wait for the steam in the pressure cooker to get released naturally.

Most loved accompaniments with Khichdi: Dahi, Ghee, Achaar & Papad

ANDHRA PRADESH

Masoor or Moong Dal Khichdi is typically made by natives of Andhra Pradesh. We like it more when it's made with Masoor Dal!

TASTING NOTES
Mint leaves add a nice depth to flavour

SERVES 5-6	SOAK TIME 30 MINS	COOK TIME 20 MINS

METHOD

1 cup basmati/normal rice (soak for 30 min)
½ cup masoor dal/moong dal (soak for 30 min)
1 thinly sliced onion
3 green chillies chopped
1 tsp ginger garlic paste
2 bay leaves
1 inch cinnamon
4 cloves
4 cardamom
½ tsp black pepper
½ tsp shahi jeera
5 sprigs mint leaves
¼ cup chopped coriander
1 tsp ghee
Salt to taste
¼ tsp turmeric powder
3-4 tbsp oil
3 cups water

- Heat oil in a pressure cooker and add whole spices.
- Once jeera crackles, add onions, green chillies and sauté until soft and light brown.
- Add ginger garlic paste, turmeric powder and fry for a minute.
- Add water, salt, mint leaves, coriander leaves, ghee and mix well.
- Add rice, cover and cook for 3 whistles or till rice is perfectly done.

ARUNACHAL PRADESH

Also known as Kharzi, this North Eastern khichdi is one of our favorites because it's got cheese!

TASTING NOTES

Creamy taste with a hint of spice. Green peas add freshness.

SERVES 2	SOAK TIME 15 MINS	COOK TIME 15 MINS

METHOD

2 cups Cooked rice
3-4 Dry red chillies (soak in water for 10 min)
2 tbsp Mozzarella cheese
1 tbsp Ginger
3-4 cloves Garlic
1 Tomato sliced
Salt to taste
1/2 cup Spring Onion (Bulb & Greens)
1/4 cup boiled Green peas
1 tsp Cooking oil

- Blend tomato, soaked red chillies, garlic, ginger, mozzarella cheese, salt to paste.
- In a vessel, add oil along with tomato cheese paste and saute on a very low flame.
- Keep stirring continuously to prevent the melted cheese from sticking to the bottom. Add spring onions immediately and mix for a few seconds. Once done, turn off the stove.
- Add rice, peas and mix well.
- Serve Kharzi hot with Mooli Raita (radish raita)

CHEF VICKY RATNANI

Celebrated Indian Chef, TV Personality, Author of Vicky Goes Veg
Ancient Grains Khichdi with Mango Olive salsa

TASTING NOTES

Earthy taste from different grains used. Mango salsa makes it tangy and spicy taste

SERVES 2	SOAK TIME 6 HRS	COOK TIME 15 MINS

METHOD

1/3 cup Lobhia
1/3 cup Black Rice
1/3 Cup Proso Millet
1/3 Cup Red Rice
1/3 cup Horse Gram
½ Cup Chopped Onions
1 Tbsp Chopped Ginger
1 Tbsp Chopped Garlic
1 Tbsp Chopped Green Chilies
2 Cups Tomato Puree
Mint Leaves
Coriander Leaves
3 Tbsp Olive Oil
1 Tsp Asafoetida
12 Curry Leaves
3 Tsp Cumin Seeds
1 Cinnamon Stick
1 Bay Leaf
1 Tsp Turmeric
1 Tsp Red Chili Powder
1 Litre Vegetable Stock
Any veg from the fridge cut into cubes

For Mango olive Salsa
1 mango cut into cubes
Chopped Olives
1 tbsp Chopped Onions
2 tbsp Chopped tomatoes
Lemon Juice
1 Tbsp Olive Oil
1 Tbsp Chopped Fresh Coriander
1 Tsp Green Chillies

- Soak the grains and lentils in water for 6 hours
- In a pan, heat oil and add the cumin seeds, curry leaves, asafoetida, red chili powder, turmeric and fry for 1 minute
- Add the onions, ginger, garlic and chili paste and cook for 2 minutes
- Add all the grains and the lentils and mix well
- Add the chopped tomatoes along with the stock and cook until the lentils and rice are almost over cooked
- Add the coconut milk , and adjust the seasoning with salt and pepper
- Garnish with chopped mint and coriander.
- Mix all Salsa ingredients in a bowl, season to taste and serve with raita, pickle and papad.

Chef Vicly Ratnani's Khichdi

ASSAM

This multi dal khichdi is made with a medley of three dals and rice

TASTING NOTES

Mixed dals give a wholesome flavour and the tempering adds spicy warmth

SERVES 4-5	SOAK TIME 60 MINS	COOK TIME 20 MINS

METHOD

1 cup Rice soaked
1/2 cup Masoor dal soaked
1/2 cup Aarhar dal soaked
1/2 cup Moong dal soaked
Salt to taste
½ tsp Turmeric
1 Green chillies (optional)
1 tsp Ginger-garlic paste
1 Bay leaf
7 Cup water

For tempering
3 to 4 Garlic Cloves (roughly crushed)
3 to 4 Dry Chilli
A pinch of Hing
1 tsp Red Chilli Powder
Few Curry Leaves
½ tsp Whole Cumin
½ tsp Mustard Seeds
1 Small Onion finely chopped
3 tsp Mustard Oil

- In a pressure cooker, put all the dals, rice, salt, turmeric, bay leaf, green chilli, ginger-garlic paste and water. Give four to five whistles or till it is properly cooked.
- For the tempering, heat oil in a pan and add onion, garlic and dry chilies. Fry till onions and garlic turn slightly brown, add cumin seeds, mustard seeds and curry leaves. Once the whole spices make a popping sound add the red chilli powder. Finally, add the hing and pour the tempering to khichdi.
- Serve hot with ghee.

Assam's Khichdi

GOA

This Goan khichdi, also known as Gud Nariyal Khichdi makes for a delicious Konkani dessert

TASTING NOTES

Sweet, earthy cardamom taste.
Coconut gives it a nice coastal feel

SERVES 2	SOAK TIME 30 MINS	COOK TIME 25 MINS

METHOD

1/2 Cup Rice (sona masuri) soaked
1/2 Cup Moong dal soaked
11/2 + 3/4 Cup water
1 Cup Powdered jaggery
1/2 Cup Grated coconut
1 tbsp Cardamom powder
5 tbsp Ghee
2 tbsp Raisins
2 tbsp Fried cashews

- Pressure cook rice and dal with 11/2 cups of water for 1 whistle or until they are cooked through.
- In a nonstick pan, add jaggery with ¾ cup water and boil till it dissolves. Add grated coconut, mix well and simmer for a minute or two.
- Add pressure cooked khichdi to it and mix well.
- Simmer until the mixture dries up completely and starts leaving the pan
- Add in ghee, raisins, cashews and mix well.
- Remove the khichdi off heat and serve it hot or cold with loads of ghee on top.

Miss Raageshwari Loomba
Singer, Actress, Television Personality, Mindfulness Speaker
Super sweet and always ready to help

It's funny how, as a child, I associated Khichdi with bad health because, let's face it, be it the seasonal fever or monsoon cough, we were all served hot Khichdi with a dollop of ghee to cure our bodies. In fact, when there was no time to cook, our mothers and grandmothers would choose to prepare Khichdi as it is a one-pot quick meal to make. But in all honesty, this preparation of rice and moong dal has given me so many memories to cherish forever.

Now that I'm old enough to understand the benefits of Khichdi and relish its taste, I value this simple meal more than ever. The smell of its jeera tadka is something that often follows me when I'm thousands of miles away from home. Just like the soulful chicken soup of the West, I strongly feel that our desi Khichdi is also a complete hearty meal.

Over the years, we've witnessed Khichdi undergoing intensive makeovers. With those colourful veggies added to its staple recipe, it has now become modern to suit the taste of the younger generation. For example, recently, I happened to try a Khichdi that almost looked like a stew! It goes without saying that it was equally comforting and delicious.

Back home, my mother enjoys experimenting with Khichdi every now and then. A couple of months ago, she made it with mutton keema, rice, and different kinds of dals. Interestingly, she mixed chana dal, moong dal, toor dal and arhar dal with a wonderful array of vegetables like peas, bell peppers, etc. The special tempering was done with finely chopped ginger, garlic, onions and tomatoes in homemade ghee. The result was scrumptious to say the least. When I asked her the secret behind the unforgettable taste that I'm missing terribly in London, she said it was the ancient method of slow-cooking that did the magic.

Trust me when I say it doesn't matter whether your Khichdi is vegetarian or non-vegetarian or if you cook it in a pressure cooker or a pot. What's important is that you savour it with an open heart without considering it a 'food for patients!'

With this, I also want to take the opportunity to break the myth that eating Khichdi is like inviting more calories on your plate. The traditional khichdi, which is made using moong dal, is, in fact, a rich source of protein and fibre that helps keep our digestion strong and our stomach fuller for a long time. Please don't think that because of rice, it's an unhealthy dish. It is a perfect way to balance proteins and carbs in your daily diet. To make your Khichdi even more nutritive, one can add more veggies to its recipe or switch water with coconut milk - a common style of cooking in South India. How diverse!

Let me end this note by thanking my mother, Veera, because of whom I've grown so fond of Khichdi today. I love it when my mother comes to London and makes me Khichdi. That's our way of celebrating 'home' together!

GUJARAT

This simple and tasty moong dal ni khichdi is made in most Gujarati households

TASTING NOTES

Soothing taste with a hint of hing

SERVES 2-3	SOAK TIME 30 MINS	COOK TIME 25 MINS

METHOD

½ cup Short grain rice soaked

½ cup Chilkewali moong dal soaked

Salt to taste

½ tsp Turmeric powder

a pinch of Hing

3 cups Water

- Take dal and rice in a pressure cooker.
- Add salt, turmeric powder and hing.
- Add water. Stir and cook for 3-4 whistles or until cooked.
- Serve hot with Gujarati kadhi.

HARYANA

Bajra matar khichdi is the Haryanvi variant of khichdi mostly made in winters and has a twist of matar in it

TASTING NOTES

Slightly chewy texture with a spicy aftertaste.

SERVES 3-4	SOAK TIME 8 HRS	COOK TIME 20 MINS

METHOD

1 cup Bajra soaked overnight

1 cup Moong dal soaked for 30 min

1/2 cup Green peas

1/2 tsp Asafoetida

1/2 tsp Turmeric powder

1 tsp Cumin seeds

1/2 tsp Cumin powder

1/2 tsp Garam masala powder

1-2 Dried red chillies

2-3 Green chillies (optional)

1 tbsp Ghee

Salt to taste

- In a pressure cooker, add bajra, moong dal, salt and water.
- Pressure cook for 5 whistles.
- Heat ghee in a pan and add cumin seeds, heeng, dried red chillies, turmeric powder, cumin powder and garam masala powder.
- Add peas and cook for 2-3 minutes on low flame.
- Add boiled bajra-dal mix to the tempering.
- Serve hot.

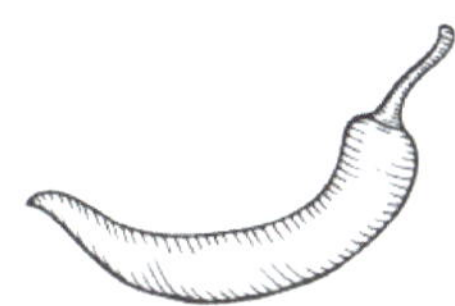

HIMACHAL PRADESH

Balaee, the khichdi from Himachal Pradesh is loaded with protein of Kala chana

TASTING NOTES

Slightly sour tasting, chewy khichdi.

SERVES 2	SOAK TIME 1 HR	COOK TIME 30 MINS

METHOD

1 cup Rice soaked
2/3 cup Kala Chana soaked overnight
1 large Onion thinly sliced
3 cups Buttermilk
2 tsp Coriander Seeds
¾ tsp Cumin Seeds
1/3 tsp Fenugreek Seeds
½ tsp Red Chilli Powder
¼ tsp Turmeric Powder
2 tsp Ghee
Salt to Taste

- For the Masala, dry roast coriander, cumin, and fenugreek till the color gets a little dark. Grind into a fine powder after it cools.
- Heat ghee in a pressure cooker.
- Add onions and 1/4 tsp salt, Fry till the onion turns light brown.
- Add the masala powder, red chilli powder, turmeric and mix well.
- Add rice and kala chana, saute for few minutes
- Add the buttermilk and adjust salt. Mix well.
- Pressure cook for 4 whistles.
- Serve Balaee hot with a generous dollop of white butter.

CHEF ALTAMASH PATEL

Executive chef – Oakwood Premier Prestige Bangalore, Promising Chef 2021
Protein Khichdi

TASTING NOTES
Chewy, spicy chunky texture

SERVES
2

SOAK TIME
30 MINS

COOK TIME
15 MINS

METHOD

Ghee

20 gms Rice (washed &
soaked for 30 mins)

1 cup Soya chunks

1 cup Onion sliced

1 Green chili chopped

1 Tomato chopped

Salt to taste

1 tbsp Garam masala

1/2 tbsp Red chili powder

- In a pressure cooker, heat ghee.
- Sauté onion chillies & tomatoes.
- Once fragrant, add rice & soya chunks.
- Sauté & add masalas.
- Add 3 cups of water & cook for 3 whistles.
- Once steam releases, open & mix.
- Garnish with lemon wedge & coriander.
- Serve hot.

JAMMU & KASHMIR

Also known as Mongkhasar, moong masoor khichdi is made with aromatic Kashmiri spices

TASTING NOTES

Robust flavour of spices with garlicky aftertaste. Warm and comforting

SERVES 2	SOAK TIME 1 HR	COOK TIME 20 MINS

METHOD

1/2 Cup Rice soaked
1/4 Cup Masoor dal soaked
1/4 Cup chilkewali Moong dal soaked
2-3 tbsp Mustard oil
1 inch Cinnamon stick
2-3 Green cardamoms
5-6 Cloves
1-2 Bay leaves
1 tsp Cumin seeds
1 Onion, sliced
1 tbsp Ginger-garlic paste
Salt to taste
1/2 tsp Turmeric powder
1 tsp Coriander powder
1 tsp Cumin powder
1 tsp Fennel powder
1-2 Green chilies
1 tsp Sugar
1 tsp Butter / ghee
1/2 tsp Garam masala powder
1 tsp Dry mint leaves, crushed
1-2 tbsp Coriander leaves, chopped
4 cups Water

- Heat oil in a pan. Temper with cumin seeds, bay leaves, cinnamon, cardamoms and cloves. Saute for a few seconds.
- Add the onions and fry till light brown. Next, add the ginger-garlic paste, turmeric powder, red chili powder, coriander powder, cumin powder and fennel powder. Mix everything well and saute for a minute.
- Add the soaked lentils, green chilies and salt. Give it a stir and continue to fry for 2 minutes.
- Add water and bring it to a boil. Cover and simmer on a medium flame. Keep stirring from time to time. Cook until soft and the water has almost evaporated.
- Add the butter / ghee, garam masala powder, mint powder and coriander leaves.
- Serve with curd.

Jammu & Kashmir's Khichdi

KARNATAKA

This traditional yellow Moong dal khichdi is made with a robust Elaichi cinnamon tadka

TASTING NOTES

Creamy texture with a hint of warm spiced heat

SERVES 4	SOAK TIME 30 MINS	COOK TIME 30 MINS

METHOD

1 cup Rice soaked
1 cup Moong Dal soaked
1 tsp Turmeric powder
1 Cardamom
3-4 cloves
1 inch Cinnamon Stick
1 tbsp Ghee
5 cups water

- Pressure cook rice and moong dal with water, salt and turmeric for about 3 whistles.
- Heat ghee in a pan and add cinnamon, cloves and cardamom to crackle and pour it over the khichdi.
- Serve hot.

Karnatka's Khichdi

KERALA

This typical Kerala red rice khichdi is enriched with antioxidants & minerals

TASTING NOTES

Wholesome chewy khichdi with spicy and sour taste

SERVES 2-3	SOAK TIME 30 MINS	COOK TIME 30 MINS

METHOD

1 cup Broken Red Rice
¾ cup Arhar Dal
1 cup French Beans 1" pieces
½ cup Carrots cubed
1 medium size Potato cubed
1 cup Brinjal cubed
3 medium size Tomatoes chopped
½ cup Shallots
3-4 Green Chillies slit lengthwise
1 sprig Curry leaves
1 tsp Turmeric Powder
1 tbsp Chilli Powder (optional)
1 tbsp Tamarind pulp
1 tsp Mustard seeds
1 tsp Jeera
2 tbsp Oil
Salt to taste
5 cups water

- In a pressure cooker, add the rice, dal and water.
- Bring to a boil. Add the shallots, tomatoes, chillies, french beans, carrots, potato, brinjal along with the turmeric powder, chilli powder and salt
- Pressure cook the rice, dal and vegetables for 4 whistles or until done.
- Heat oil in a pan, add the mustard seeds, jeera and the curry leaves. Add this tempering mixture to the cooked khichdi and put the cooker back on heat.
- Add the tamarind pulp. Allow it to simmer for 5 minutes.
- Serve hot.

Random Khichdi pictures

Makhani Khichdi

Tandoori Paneer Khichdi

MADHYA PRADESH

Sabudana khichdi is made with tapioca. The crunchy peanuts make this dish so yummy!

TASTING NOTES

Sticky spicy khichdi with crunchy peanuts

SERVES 2	SOAK TIME 3-4 HRS	COOK TIME 20 MINS

METHOD

1 cup Sabudana soaked for
1 hour, drained for 2 hours
1 medium Potato cubed
2 Green chillies chopped
2 tbsp Coriander leaves
chopped
Some Curry leaves
1 tsp Cumin seeds
1 tsp Red chilli powder
1 tsp Garam masala
1 tsp Coriander powder
Salt to taste
4 tbsp Ghee
1/4 Cup Peanuts

- Heat ghee in a pan and fry the peanuts till crispy, keep aside.
- In the same pan, add jeera, ginger and curry leaves. Saute for a minute.
- Add potato and cover the lid, cook on low heat till potatoes are done.
- Add sabudana and fried peanuts. Mix and add salt, red chilli powder, garam masala, coriander powder. Cook for a minute.
- Garnish with coriander leaves.
- Serve hot with curd.

Madhya Pradesh's Khichdi

Shubra Chatterji
Co-Founder Tonsvalleyshop
Food Historian

I've spent the larger part of the last ten years travelling around India, shooting food (and eating it too) in every street and alley-way, at every kind of eatery – from road-side carts to palace-hotels with centuries of history attached to them, and in hundreds of homes like yours and mine, urban and rural, by the sea, cocooned in forests, or perched atop mountains. But as we pack-up the day's shoot, gather our cameras and ourselves and make our way to unfamiliar hotel-rooms, or motel rooms, a gentle longing for familiarity sets in. What makes an impersonal hotel-room home? I make sure to put out my favourite teas and coffees by the tea-service, and books on my bedside table. But is that enough? People tell me they envy my life, and I too wouldn't have it any other way. But when you've been on the road for months on end, you long for a piece of home. This is why, Khichdi. Khichdi to me is an instant ticket to what feels like home. I have so many moments I can recall putting that first spoonful of a room- service ordered dish in my mouth, eyes shut, and being transported home. Khichdi speaks straight to my soul.

Apart from seeing me through many a day or night far away from home, it is a perfect cooker-full of khichdi that my now-husband cooked for me before we were even dating that made me decide that this shall be the man I marry. I kid you not. His khichdi, different from mine, had whole potatoes with skin on cubed into it, and roughly quartered tomatoes, and was topped with a generous spoonful of pahadi ghee which did the trick. I was at home once again.

Chef Jyoti Vishnani
Masterchef India Contestant
Also known as 'Chulbuli Chef'

My memories of khichdi take me back to my childhood with my grandmother. She used to tell lovely stories around Khichdi. For me, khichdi means comfort, a warm hug and nostalgia. In sindhi household, khichdi is accompanied by turai or dal turai, fried potatoes (Tariyal Patata), curd and papad. My grandma used to have khichdi with gajar ka achar which is a water-based pickled with yellow mustard and green garlic, something similar to kanji.

I love my khichdi with veggies and accompanied with curd and lemon pickle. Whenever I travel somewhere and back home, this is the first thing I crave for.

SAEE KORANNE KHANDEKAR

Culinary Consultant, Maharashtrian Food Expert
This Masoor khichdi is from the North coastal belt of the Konkan

TASTING NOTES

Coconutty Spicy Flavour

SERVES 2

SOAK TIME 30 MINS

COOK TIME 20 MINS

METHOD

1/2 cup Whole Masoor
1 cup short grain rice such as
AmbeMohor or Indrayani
1 small Onion finely chopped
3 cloves Garlic
1/2 inch Ginger
1 tbsp Coriander stems roughly
chopped
1/2 tbsp Fresh green coriander
roughly chopped
2 tbsp Fresh or dried grated
coconut
1 small Green chili
3-4 Peppercorns
1/4 inch Cinnamon or cassia bark
6-8 Curry leaves
2 tbsp Ghee
1/2 tsp Cumin seeds
Large pinch of Asafoetida
1/4 tsp Turmeric powder
1 tsp Coriander seed powder
Salt to taste
1/2 tsp Sugar
1 tsp CKP masala

- Wash and drain the rice and masoor.
- Place the coconut, coriander stem, coriander leaves, ginger, garlic, green chili, peppercorn and cinnamon in a blender and blend to a coarse paste without adding any water.
- Heat ghee in a heavy bottomed pot or pressure cooker.
- To this, add the cumin seeds, asafoetida, turmeric powder, and curry leaves.
- When the curry leaves splutter, add the onions and sauté briefly until the raw smell disappears.
- Tip in the drained rice and lentils. Roast patiently over a low flame until they feel light.
- Add salt, sugar, CKP masala and coriander seed powder. Roast for a further two minutes.
- Add 3 cups of water and cook covered until soft (or pressure cook for one whistle, turn the heat to sim for 8 minutes and then turn off the flame, allowing the pressure to release naturally.)
- Serve hot with a drizzle of ghee and a garnish of coconut and coriander.

MAHARASHTRA

Maharashtrian masala khichdi has Khandeshi masala which takes the taste to the next level.

TASTING NOTES

Spicy, crunchy and tropical flavour with a garlicky aftertaste

SERVES 2	SOAK TIME 30 MINS	COOK TIME 20 MINS

METHOD

1 cup Rice soaked
1/3 cup Arhar dal soaked
2 medium Onion sliced
2 tbsp Garlic
¼ cup Dried coconut
¼ cup peanuts
3 tbsp Khandeshi garam masala
½ tsp Turmeric
Salt to taste
2 ¼ cup Water
2 tbsp Cilantro / Coriander leaves
¼ cup Groundnut oil

- Combine dried coconut and garlic in a grinder and make a fine paste.
- Heat oil in a pressure cooker, add onions and sauté it until it changes color.
- Add grinded paste and Sauté until the raw smell of garlic is gone.
- Add the Khandeshi garam masala and turmeric. Mix well and sauté for a minute.
- When the oil begins to separate, add the peanuts and sauté for another minute.
- Finally, add the rice, arhar dal and salt. Roast in spices for 2-3 minutes
- Add water and cook for 4 whistles or until done.
- Garnish it with finely chopped fresh coriander leaves.
- Serve hot.

MANIPUR

Manipuri Black rice khichdi has a hint of ghondharaj lebu which changes the game

TASTING NOTES

Tangy flavour with lemon garlic taste

SERVES 2-3	SOAK TIME 1 HR	COOK TIME 15 MINS

METHOD

1 cup Manipuri Black rice soaked

1.5 cups Moong dal soaked

2 tbsp Ghee

½ tsp Panch Phoran

1-2 pcs Dried bay leaf

4-5 pcs Gondhoraj lebu leaf

1 Green chilli slit lengthwise

1 tbsp Ginger chopped

1 tbsp Garlic sliced

4-5 cups Chicken/vegetable stock

1-2 cups Tomato blanched, peeled and chopped

1 tsp Turmeric powder

Salt to taste

- Heat ghee in a pan, add the Panch Phoran, dried bay leaf, green chilli, ginger and garlic.
- Add the tomatoes and turmeric and cook for about 3-5 mins till all the water has evaporated and tomatoes form a nice paste
- Add rice and dal and mix well
- Add the stock, the lemon leaves and check for seasoning.
- Cook till dal and rice soft
- Garnish with more ghee and coriander.
- Serve hot.

MEGHALAYA

Meghalayan Jadoh is a non vegetarian khichdi made with local rice

TASTING NOTES

Wholesome meaty texture with peppery taste

SERVES 2-3	SOAK TIME 1 HR	COOK TIME 30 MINS

METHOD

2 cups Joha rice washed
300 gm Pork (with fat) cut into 1/2" cubes
1 medium Onion chopped
1 tbsp Ginger paste
1/2 tsp Turmeric powder
1 tsp ground Black pepper
2 Bay leaves
2 tbsp Vegetable oil
Salt to taste
4 cups Water
Fresh coriander for garnish

- Heat oil in a pan. Add the onions, ginger paste, turmeric and black pepper and fry till the oil separates.
- Burn the tip of the bay leaves and immediately drop in the pan. Add the pork pieces and fry for sometime till light brown.
- Add rice and fry for 2-3 minutes. Add salt.
- Add water and simmer till cooked.
- Garnish with coriander and serve with fermented soya paste (Tungrymbai) and Dohneiiong (pork with sesame seeds).

MIZORAM

Bai is a North-Eastern dal-less khichdi made with rice and vegetables

TASTING NOTES

Warm spiced buttery consistency, overcooked texture

SERVES 3-4	SOAK TIME 30 MINS	COOK TIME 15 MINS

METHOD

1 cup Rice
3 cup Mixed vegetables(leafy vegetable, cauliflower, carrot, beans & potatoes)

3 Green chilli
5 cups Water
Salt to taste
3 tsp Cooking soda

- Boil water, add salt and cooking soda, till the bubbles subside.
- Add stalks, leaves and a few florets of a small cauliflower, chopped beans, green chilli, rice and potato.
- Cook in a low heat, adding more water as required, until the rice, potatoes and beans are cooked.
- Serve hot.

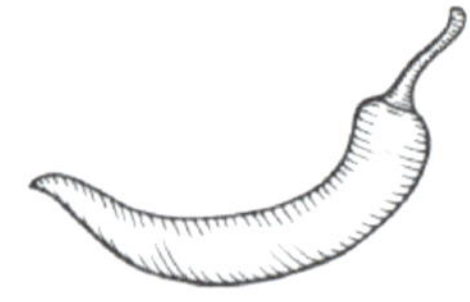

Mizoram's Khichdi

NAGALAND

Galho is a treat for Axone or fermented soybean lovers

TASTING NOTES

Very strong fermented flavour, an acquired taste

SERVES 2	SOAK TIME 30 MINS	COOK TIME 1 HR

METHOD

2 cups Pumpkin/squash leaves (or any green leafy vegetable)

¾ cup Rice

1 tbsp of Axone (Fermented Soybean)

Salt to taste

1 kg Smoked Pork chopped

2 Green chillies chopped

1 cup Water

- Put water, axone and green chillies into a pot and cook it for 5 minutes. Add salt to taste.
- Add smoked pork into the pot and cook it for another 45 minutes or more until the meat becomes tender
- Put in the rice. Add in more water if required.
- After the rice is almost done, add the chopped greens
- Let it simmer for 5-7 mins.
- Serve hot.

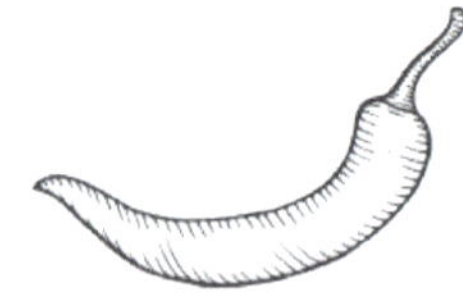

ORISSA

Popular as Jagannath puri ki khichdi, this khichdi is served as 'prasad' in Orissa. That definitely enhances the taste!

TASTING NOTES

Hearty ginger warmth, comforting ghee flavour

SERVES 2-3	SOAK TIME 30 MINS	COOK TIME 30 MINS

METHOD

6 to 10 sprigs Cilantro leaves
2 tbsp Cumin seeds
1 cup Ghee
4 cups Water boiled
3 tbsp Ginger minced
1 tbsp Hing
1 Fresh shredded coconut
½ cup saboot moong dal
2 cups Rice
A few Raisins

- Heat ghee in a pan, add cumin seeds and allow them to sizzle and immediately add into the boiling water.
- Add rice, moong dal, coconut, ginger, hing and raisins.
- Cover and cook, stir in between.
- After 15 mins rice will be ready. Add chopped cilantro and rest of the ghee.

PUNJAB

This Punjabi Choliya di khichdi is a simple everyday khichdi with chana dal

---

TASTING NOTES

Mild tasting khichdi with soothing effect

SERVES 2	SOAK TIME 30 MINS	COOK TIME 20 MINS

METHOD

1/2 cup Chana Dal soaked
1/2 cup Basmati rice soaked
pinch of Hing
1/2 tsp Red chilli powder
1 tbsp Ghee
Salt to taste
2 cups water

- Heat ghee in the pressure cooker and add the red chili powder, asafoetida and salt. Stir and fry for a few seconds.
- Add the chana dal, stir and add water.
- Pressure cook for 2 whistles or until done. Once the pressure settles down on its own, remove the lid.
- Once cooked add the rice and again pressure cook for 1 or 2 whistles. Dal would cook further along with the rice.
- Specialty of this khichdi is the separate grains of rice and dal and it's not mushy or pasty. if the rice is not cooked, then you can add about 1/8 to 1/4 cup water and pressure cook again for a whistle or two.
- Serve hot with yogurt or raita.

RAJASTHAN

Add some onions to Rajasthani Moong dal ri khichdi to it to make it more appealing!

TASTING NOTES

Home style khichdi that tastes like childhood

SERVES 2-3	SOAK TIME 1 HR	COOK TIME 20 MINS

METHOD

1 cup chilka Moong dal soaked
1 cup Rice soaked
½ tsp Jeera Seeds
1 tsp Garam Masala Powder
1 tsp Chilli Powder
3 Big Cardamom
2 pcs Cinnamon
¾ tbsp Ginger finely chopped
2 Onion chopped
2 tbsp Oil
Salt to taste

- Heat half of the oil in a pressure cooker and add Jeera, Big Cardamom, Cinnamon and fry for a few minutes.
- Add Ginger, Garam Masala, Chilli Powder and fry for 2 to 3 minutes.
- Once done, add Rice and dal, and cook for 2 minutes.
- Add Water and Salt, Mix well.
- Pressure cook for about 3 to 4 whistles. After that, allow it to release the pressure for a few minutes.
- Heat remaining oil in a small frying pan, add onions and fry until it becomes transparent.
- Add fried onion to the khichdi and mix well.
- Khichdi should be watery, if it is too thick add little hot water and mix well.
- Serve hot.

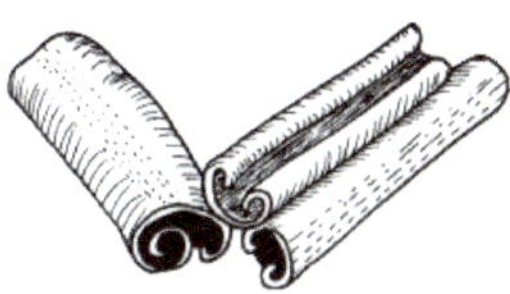

SIKKIM

*Sikkimese Chambray is another dal less khichdi
from our cauldron*

TASTING NOTES

A pulao kind khichdi, cumin enhances the taste

SERVES 2	SOAK TIME 15 MINS	COOK TIME 20 MINS

METHOD

1 cup Basmati Rice soaked
½ inch Cinnamon
Pinch of Turmeric powder
Salt to taste
1 Bay leaf
2 tsp Ghee
¼ tsp Black Cumin Seed
1 ½ cup Water

- Heat ghee in a non-stick pan, add cinnamon, bay leaf, cumin seeds, let it splutter. Then add the rice, Fry for 2 mins.
- Add turmeric and salt. Mix well and add water. Cover with lid and cook in sim for 10 mins or till the rice is cooked.
- Chambray is eaten with Til ko alu.

CHEF IZZAT HUSSAIN

Unani Physician & Indian, Mughlai Chef
Cooks mouthwatering food without water

TASTING NOTES

Buttery khichdi with strong kalounji flavour

SERVES 2-3	SOAK TIME 30 MINS	COOK TIME 15 MINS

METHOD

100 gms Arhar dal
150 gms Rice washed,
soaked for 30 minutes
350 gm water
1/2 tsp Kalounji seeds
1/2 tsp Black pepper
50 gm Butter
A few Green chillies
Salt to taste.

- Take a bowl & mix everything together.
- Put in the microwave for 10 minutes.
- After 10 minutes stir well and keep again in the microwave for 5 minutes only.
- Serve hot.

TAMIL NADU

*How about we make a khichdi without dal or rice? Intrigued?
Try this delicious rawa khichdi from Tamil Nadu!*

TASTING NOTES

Wholesome veg upma style khichdi

SERVES 2	SOAK TIME 30 MINS	COOK TIME 20 MINS

METHOD

1 cup Sooji
3 tbsp Ghee
1 tsp Mustard seeds
1 tsp Chana Dal
1 tsp Urad Dal
1/2 cup Onions
10 Curry leaves
2 Chillies
1/2 tsp Ginger
1/4th cup Carrots
1/4th cup Green peas
1/2 cup Tomatoes
1/2 tsp Turmeric
3 cups Water
Salt to taste
Coriander leaves to garnish

- Dry roast sooji in a hot pan till it changes color and you get a nice aroma. Keep aside once done.
- Heat ghee in a pan & add mustard seeds.
- Add chana dal & Urad dal.
- Add onions, chilli, ginger, curry leaves and fry for 2-3 minutes.
- Add carrot, peas, tomatoes & mix.
- Add haldi, water & boil.
- Slowly mix sooji so that no lumps are formed.
- Mix well & cook covered for 3 minutes.
- Serve with lemon wedge & coconut chutney.

Tamilnadu's Khichdi

TRIPURA

Bhangui khichdi has boiled conical parcels which make it appealing for both eyes and palette!

TASTING NOTES

Sticky texture with strong ginger flavour

SERVES 3-4	SOAK TIME 30 MINS	COOK TIME 1 HR

METHOD

1 kg White flavored sticky rice (Binni rice/ Govindobhog Rice) wash & dried

1 cup Ghee

2 pcs Onion sliced

2-3 inch Ginger chopped

Salt to taste

5 Bhangui / Banana leaf

1 litre water

- Mix ghee with rice, onion, ginger and salt.
- Make a cone shape with Bhangui / Banana leaf and pour the rice without leaving any space.
- Tie the leaves tightly.
- Dip all the cone-tied preparation in water and boil them for an hour or until done.
- Serve with some fish fry, egg fry or any fried item.

Kalyan Karmarkar
Blogger – TheFinelyChopped
Loving Cat Dad to Baby Loaf & Little Nimki

To me khichuri is all about reliving childhood memories of having it in the Durga puja pandal on Ashtami and at home on rainy days in Kolkata. I often make it in Mumbai as I find it to be a simple, one dish meal to make.

At times I have it with fish fry or an omelette. I add vegetables to it too. I love the occasions when I can go to Durga Pujas in Mumbai and have khichuri. Khichuri is love.

Chef Saby Gorai
The Urban Chef
President of Young Chefs
Awarded 'Best Chef of India' by The President of India

My most fond memories of khichdi are from my childhood whenever there was a rain in the neighborhood and my mum would make khichdi and we would all look forward to it. This is a very typical Bengali tradition of making khichdi on rainy days and it is a yellow dal khichdi made with a lot of vegetables. It's nothing like the khichdi we make in the north which is generally used as a food for people who are sick or recovering patients. This is something unique and extremely tasty and eventually it is served with an egg omelette or other fried vegetables on the side and it is like a full meal.

Khichdi also happens to be the best one pot meal full of nutrition with local vegetable seasonal ingredients. It is extremely easy to make, healthy and a sustainable dish considering today's scenario.It could be made with almost all combinations of rice dal vegetables also with other cereals, pulses, millets, Jwaar, Bajra, ragi, barley etc. and various other other pulses cereals and grains along with seasonal vegetables to make a beautiful khichadi.

Currently my favourite is a millet khichdi which I make with mixed millet and seasonal vegetables and pulses. It is an extremely flavourful and tasty one pot dish and can be eaten anytime at lunch or dinner and it is a complete meal on its own(one can add eggs/chicken/ meat to make it protein rich).

UTTAR PRADESH

Uttar Pradeshi Saboot Masoor ki khichdi is one of our most favorite khichdis!

TASTING NOTES

Peppery creamy khichdi with fragrance of spices

SERVES 2-3	SOAK TIME 15 MINS	COOK TIME 20 MINS

METHOD

½ cup Sabot masoor soaked
1 ½ cup Rice soaked
4 tbsp Ghee
1 tsp Cumin seeds
5-6 Black peppercorns
2 Cloves
1 inch Cinnamon
1 inch Ginger finely chopped
2 Green chillies finely chopped
¼ tsp Turmeric powder
Salt to taste
4 cups water

- Heat ghee in a non-stick pan, add cumin seeds, black peppercorns, cloves, cinnamon and sauté until fragrant.
- Add ginger, green chillies and sauté for a minute.
- Add rice and dal, turmeric powder, salt and water.
- Cover and cook on medium heat till done.
- Serve hot with a drizzle of ghee.

Uttar Pradesh's Khichdi

WEST BENGAL

This super tasty Bhogerkhichudi is served as 'prasad'
in West Bengal

TASTING NOTES

Hearty mustard flavoured khichdi

SERVES 2	SOAK TIME 30 MINS	COOK TIME 30 MINS

METHOD

1 cup Basmati rice washed & dried
½ cup Moong dal washed & dried
½ cup Water
6 tbsp Oil
1 tbsp Ginger (grated)
½ tsp Turmeric powder
1 tsp Jeera powder
1 tbsp Mustard oil
2 Bay leaves
1 Cinnamon
2 Cloves
2 Dried red chillies
1 tsp Jeera
2 tbsp Grated coconut
1 Tomato (cut into quarter)
1 Potato (peeled and cut into big cubes)
8-10 pcs Cauliflower (cut into big florets)
1 Green chilli (slit)
1 ½ litres Hot water
½ cup Green peas
2 tsp Sugar
1 tbsp Ghee
Bengali garam masala (Roast & Grind)
3 one-inch stickCinnamon sticks
4 Cardamom
5 Cloves

- Add moong dal in a heated pan & dry roast for 2-3 minutes, until it turns brown.
- Add a tablespoon of oil in a heated pan & roast dried rice for 1-2 minutes. Keep it aside.
- Mix ginger, turmeric powder & jeera powder. Keep it aside.
- Heat mustard oil in a pan. Add the bay leaves, dried red chillies, cinnamon stick, two cloves, jeera and sauté well.
- Add coconut and mix well for 2 minutes. Add the ginger paste and sauté for another minute. Add tomato and stir well for 2 minutes and remove it from the stove.
- Heat 4 tbsp oil in a big pan and add the moong dal, rice split green chilli, salt, hot water and cover and cook for 5 minutes.
- Remove the lid and add the roasted tomato-coconut masala.
- Add vegetables, green peas and sugar.
- Add another half a litre of hot water and then add a teaspoon of the powdered Bengali garam masala. Mix well and cover it with the lid again.
- Allow it to cook for 15 minutes. Add a tablespoon of ghee and transfer it into a bowl.
- Serve hot.

Bhoger Khichuri by Pikturenama Studios

NITIN HAJELA
Food Critic
Food enthusiast

TASTING NOTES

*Comforting flavour of caramelized onions,
tangy tomato taste*

SERVES 2-3	SOAK TIME 1 HR	COOK TIME 20 MINS

METHOD

Basmati broken rice 1 cup
Arhar / Toor Dal 1 cup
Desi ghee
1 bay leaf
Asafetida / Hing 1 pinch
Chopped Garlic 2 pods
Cumin/ Zeera seeds
Onion chopped 1 Small size
Tomato chopped 1 Medium size
Green chilies 1 pc (optional)
Red chili powder 1 Tsp
Garam masala 1 tsp
Turmeric powder 1 tsp
Salt to taste

For Garnish
Chopped Coriander leaves
Homemade Ghee
Crispy fried brown onions

- Add 2-3 tbsp of ghee in a pressure cooker and heat on slow flame.
- Add bay leaf, cumin and asafetida and cook for a minute
- Add chopped onions till they are light brown, then add chopped garlic and green chilies and cook till rawness
- is gone.
- Add pre-soaked rice and Arhar dal to the pressure cooker and cook for a while.
- Now add red chili powder, garam masala, turmeric powder and chopped tomatoes. Cook for few minutes
- Stir and add water depending on what consistency of Khichdi you want.
- Add salt to taste. Cover lid and cook for 3-4 whistles.
- Open the lid after releasing the pressure. Use ladle to stir it so that khichdi has smooth texture and consistency.
- Garnish with lots of ghee and sprinkle with chopped coriander leaves and crispy brown fried onions.

RUSHINA MUNSHAW GHILDIYAL

Culinary Expert, Founder APB Cook studio
Passionate about regional cuisine

TASTING NOTES

Garhwali Lobia Khichdi with strong sesame flavour

SERVES 2	SOAK TIME 30 MINS	COOK TIME 20 MINS

METHOD

1 1/2 cup Basmati rice
1 cup Lobia
1/2 cup Sesame
2 tbsp Ghee
2 Bay Leaves
8 Peppercorns
4 Cloves
2 Black Cardamom
1 tbsp Cumin
Pinch of hing
1 cup Onion finely chopped
2 tbsp Garlic finely chopped
1 tbsp Green chilli finely chopped
1 tbsp Ginger grated
1 tsp Chilli powder
1 tsp Turmeric powder
1/3 cup Coriander finely chopped

- Wash and soak the Basmati rice.
- Pressure cook the Lobia in 6 cups water with salt till completely cooked. When pressed it should get smashed completely. Keep aside with cooking water.
- Meanwhile, toast the sesame until darkened. Cool and grind to a coarse powder. Keep aside.
- Drain rice and keep aside.
- Heat a large pan and add ghee.
- When hot, add the Bay Leaves, peppercorns, clove, black cardamom, cumin and heeng and saute for 30 seconds or until fragrant.
- Add the onion and saute till golden brown.
- Add the garlic and green chilli and saute 30 seconds till cooked
- Add the ginger and stir fry for 1 minute or until the raw smell is gone.
- Add the rice and saute till the rice is well coated in the spiced ghee.
- Add chilli powder, and turmeric. Saute well for 30-40 seconds.
- Add 2 cups of the Lobia cooking water, mix well and cook till rice is almost done and water is absorbed.
- Add 2 more cups of cooking water and salt to taste. Cook till the khichdi is done. The khichdi should be on the dry side with the grains separate but tender cooked.
- Stir in the sesame powder and coriander and mix well.
- Serve hot.

UTTARAKHAND

*This Urad dal khichdi is a delicious recipe by our very dear
Rushina Munshaw Ghildiyal*

TASTING NOTES

Heavily spiced, buttery khichdi

SERVES 4 | **SOAK TIME OVERNIGHT** | **COOK TIME 30 MINS**

METHOD

1 1/2 cup Basmati rice soaked
1 cup Urad Dal Sabut soaked
2 tbsp Ghee
2 Bay Leaves
8 Peppercorns
4 Cloves
2 Black Cardamoms
1 tbsp Cumin
A Pinch of Hing
1 cup Onion finely chopped
2 tbsp Garlic finely chopped
1 tbsp Green chilli finely chopped
1 tbsp Ginger grated
1 tsp Chilli powder
1 tbsp Coriander powder
1 tsp Turmeric powder
1/3 cup Coriander finely chopped
5 cups Water

- Pressure cook the Urad in 5 cups of water with salt until completely cooked. When you press it between your thumb and forefinger it should get smashed completely. Keep aside with cooking water.
- Heat ghee in a pan, add the Bay Leaves, peppercorns, clove, black cardamom, cumin and heeng and saute for 30 seconds or until fragrant.
- Add the onion and saute till golden brown.
- Add the garlic and green chilli and saute 30 seconds till cooked
- Add the ginger and stir fry for 1 minute or until the raw smell is gone.
- Add the rice and saute till the rice is well coated in the spiced ghee.
- Add chilli powder, coriander powder and turmeric. Saute well for 30–40 seconds.
- Add 2 1/2 cups of the Urad cooking water, mix well and cook till rice is almost done and water is absorbed.
- Add the cooked urad, remaining water and salt to taste and cook till the khichdi is done. Some of the water dal and rice should have broken down and there should be a bit of mushy viscosity in your khichdi.
- Stir in the coriander and mix well.
- Serve hot.

Uttarakhand's Khichdi

JHARKHAND

This sprouted dal chana khichdi from Jharkhand is a power packed masala khichdi

TASTING NOTES

Sprouted dal & chana adds nice flavour, slightly bitter taste cause of methi

SERVES 2	SOAK TIME 30 MINS	COOK TIME 30 MINS

METHOD

½ cup Moong Dal
½ cup Rice
¼ cup Sprouted Moong
¼ cup Sprouted Lal Chana
2 Tomato (chopped)
1 tsp Ginger (grated)
2 Bay leaves
1 tbsp Methi (soaked overnight)
1 tsp Whole Dhaniya
1 tsp Kitchen King powder
2 tsp Roasted Jeera powder
1 tsp Turmeric powder
Salt to taste
2 tsp Oil

For tempering
2 Dry Red Chilli
6-7 Garlic finely chopped
8-10 Curry leaves
Oil - As required

- Heat oil in a pressure cooker and add grated ginger and bay leaves.
- Add both the sprouts and fry for a few minutes.
- Add chopped tomato, salt, turmeric, kitchen king powder, rice and daal.
- Stir for a few minutes.
- Add water (a little more than double), whole dhaniya and methi.
- Pressure cook till 1 whistle. Allow the pressure to release.
- Temper with dry red chilli, garlic and curry patta.
- Serve hot with curd.

TELANGANA

Keema khichdi from the state of Telangana makes for the perfect complete meal with fiber, protein & carbs

TASTING NOTES

Wholesome meat khichdi with tangy tomato taste

SERVES 3-4	SOAK TIME 20 MINS	COOK TIME 30 MINS

1 cup Basmati rice soaked
1 cup Saboot masoor dal soaked
3 tbsp Vegetable, Canola or Sunflower oil
1 tsp Cumin seeds
1 large Onion finely chopped
1 tsp Ginger paste
2 tsp Garlic paste
2 tsp Coriander powder
1 tsp Cumin powder
1/4 tsp Turmeric powder
1 tbsp Garam masala
2 large Tomatoes finely chopped
2 cups chopped mixed vegetables of your choice
450 gms Ground meat (beef, lamb, chicken)
2 Chicken Stock cubes
Salt to taste
4 cups Water

METHOD

- Heat the oil in a pressure cooker, add the cumin seeds and cook until they stop spluttering.
- Add the chopped onions and fry until transparent.
- Add the ginger and garlic pastes and fry for 1 minute. Add the remaining spices through garam masala and mix well. Cook for 3 to 4 minutes.
- Add the tomatoes and cook until the oil begins to separate from the masala and the tomatoes turn pulpy.
- Add the ground meat and dal. Cook until the meat turns evenly brown.
- Add the vegetables, rice, stock cubes and 4 cups of water. Taste and season with salt. Mix well and bring to a boil.
- Cook for an additional 2 to 3 minutes, then lower the heat to a simmer. Put the lid on and cook until the rice and lentils get really soft, about 30 to 45 minutes. Add more water as needed to keep the mixture thoroughly moist as it cooks.
- Once the rice and lentils get soft enough to mash, turn off the heat and allow the khichdi to rest without removing the lid for 10 minutes. The khichdi should be moist and porridge-like in consistency.
- Serve hot

CHEF ANAHITA DHONDY

Former Chef Partner – SodaBottleOpenerWala,
Self Proclaimed Food Geek

TASTING NOTES

Very simple everyday comforting khichdi with gingery flavour and smooth creamy texture

SERVES 2-3	SOAK TIME 15 MINS	COOK TIME 20 MINS

METHOD

1/2 cup Rice white or brown basmati or jasmine rice
1/2 cup Mung Dal (split)
3 cups Water
1 tsp Turmeric
1 tsp Salt

- Wash and clean the rice and dal. Soak in water for 15 minutes.
- Add in a pressure cooker along with water, salt and turmeric and cook for 3 whistles. Switch off and allow the steam to come out.

For Tempering
2-3 tbsp Ghee
1 tsp Jeera
Pinch of Hing
1 tbsp chopped Ginger

- For the tadka, in a pan add ghee, jeera, heeng and ginger. Brown well and add to khichdi.
- Add some water if required and serve with achar, papad, dahi or ghee.

DELHI

Add some cashews to make this Dilli hare moong ki Khichdi addictively yummy!

TASTING NOTES

curry leaves & pepper gives this khichdi a wonderful fresh spicy taste. cashews elevate flavour

SERVES 2	SOAK TIME 2 HRS	COOK TIME 20 MINS

METHOD

3/4 cup Basmati rice
3/4 cup Sabut moong dal
1 1/2 tbsp Ghee
1 tsp Jeera
3 Cloves
1 stick Cinnamon
4 Black Peppercorns
3 Cardamoms
4 to 5 Curry leaves
2 tbsp finely chopped Onions
2 tbsp broken Cashew nuts
1 tbsp Freshly grated coconut
Salt to taste
1 tsp Green chilli paste

For Garnish
2 tbsp finely chopped
Coriander

- Heat the ghee in a pressure cooker and add the cumin seeds.
- When the seeds crackle, add the cloves, cinnamon, peppercorns, cardamom, curry leaves and onions and sauté on a medium flame for 1 to 2 minutes.
- Add the cashew nuts and sauté on a medium flame for a few seconds.
- Add the rice-moong mixture, 3 cups of hot water, coconut, salt and green chilli paste, mix well and pressure cook for 3 whistles.
- Allow the steam to escape before opening the lid.
- Garnish with coriander and serve immediately with curds, papad and pickle.

Delhi's Khichdi

Chef Ashish Bhasin
Executive Chef at the Leela Gurgaon
Named as one of the Country's Top 5 Chefs
Believes that 'A happy heart makes happy food'

Khichdi in India is the most common meal and every region has its own version. Bajra, rice, lentils, broken wheat, and sago are few of the variations in main ingredients apart from variation in flavours. Lot of people think it's a meal for patients. Yes, it's easy to digest and given to patients, but well made khichdi is a feast.

For me a well made khichdi with achaar, papad and dahi is something I relish a lot. Another khichdi which I like is bisibelebath. A fast is never complete without a sabudana khichdi. Khichuri which is made at Durga pooja has its own deliciously unique flavour which makes me stand in a queue as my heart, tongue and stomach refuse to leave the pandal.

Gurpreet Singh Tikku aka Mister Tikku
Food Blogger

Khichri naam sunte hi Mooh mein swaad aata hai. Par aisa hamesha nahi tha.

Pehle to Khichri sirf bimaari mein hi khaate the.

Par dheere dheere we started exploring Khichri and *pata laga ki* Khichri is cooked in 100 Different ways and 99 of them are delicious ones!

Aisi hi kuch Khichri recipes I got to know from CauldronSisterss ki Book, Khichri. My favourite is Dilli wali Khichri. *Usme jo Curry Patta ka flavour aaya woh bemisaal tha.*

Atul Sikand
Founder of Food Group 'Sikandalous'
Regarded one of the top most Culinary Moguls

My early childhood khichdi memories are of us cousins sitting together, probably over Sunday lunch eating our nani kay haath ki khichdi which was very basic and loaded with delicious homemade ghee, YUM !

We would sing at least once during that meal 'Khichdi ke hain chaar yaar–dahi, papad, ghee aur achar!' It was almost like a ritual that completed our cousins' feasts.

I don't associate khichdi with illness, for me it's comfort food as I think it is across India. Love it simple 'nani style' with a dollop of ghee or kickass spicy one like Karnataka's famous bisibele bath!

CHANDIGARH

As Julia Child so rightly said, "With enough butter, everything is good!", here is our Makhan wali khichdi

TASTING NOTES

Butter & red chili temper gives this khichdi a whole new spicy flavour profile

SERVES	SOAK TIME	COOK TIME
2	**30 MINS**	**30 MINS**

METHOD

½ Cup Sabut urad dal soaked
½ Cup Rice soaked
1 tsp Cumin seeds
1 Pinch of Hing
1 tbsp Vegetable oil
2 whole Dry red chilies (break them half)
Salt to taste
3 cups Water

For Hot Chilli Tadka
2 tsp crushed red chilies or red chili powder
2 tbsp melted butter or Ghee

- In a pressure cooker, heat oil, add cumin seeds and hing and fry for 2 minutes or until cumin seeds become brown.
- Add red chilies and fry them.
- Add dal, salt and water and mix,
- Pressure cook for 3-4 whistles or until dal is little cooked
- Add rice in the pressure cooker with the cooked Dal and pressure cook for another 2-3 whistles.
- Once pressure releases, serve hot with hot chilli tadka.

Chandigarh's Khichdi

SILVASSA

This Ragi vermicelli Khichdi tastes so good with dal!

TASTING NOTES

Very soothing and slightly spicy

SERVES 2	SOAK TIME 30 MINS	COOK TIME 20 MINS

METHOD

1 cup Ragi vermicelli
¼ cup Moong
1 tbsp Urad dal
1 Onion
1 Tomato
1 Green Chilli
½ tsp Mustard
½ tsp Cumin
2 tbsp Coriander leaves,
¼ tsp Turmeric powder
2 tbsp Oil
8-10 Curry Leaves
Salt to taste
1 ½ cup water

- Boil Turmeric and Moong Dal.
- Add oil to the pan and roast the mustard, urad dal, cumin, green chili and curry leaves nicely.
- Mix the roasted mixture with onion, tomato and moong dal paste which is fried and made into a paste.
- Add water, turmeric powder and salt to the prepared mixture and boil it nicely.
- Finally, add the Ragi vermicelli to the mixture, stir it well and sprinkle some coriander leaves before turning off the stove.
- Serve hot.

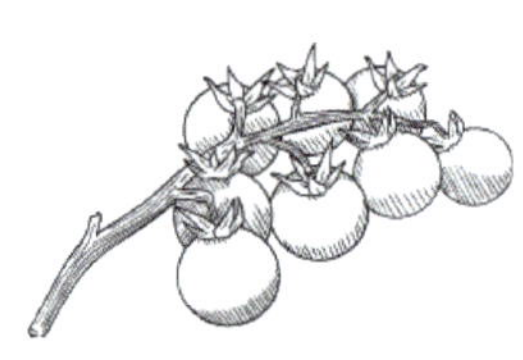

VRAT KI KHICHDI

Also known as Sama ki khichdi, Vrat ki Khichdi is a feast while you fast!

TASTING NOTES

Spicy, sour taste with crunchy texture

SERVES	SOAK TIME	COOK TIME
1	10 MINS	25 MINS

½ cup moraiyo / barnyard millet soaked
2 tbsp ghee
½ tsp cumin seeds
2 tbsp unsalted peanuts
1 green chilli, chopped finely
1 medium potato, peeled and diced
Sea salt or sendha namak (Himalayan Pink Salt)
1 cup water
½ tbsp lime or lemon juice
chopped green coriander leaves for garnish

METHOD

- Heat ghee in a pan. Add cumin seeds and saute for a moment or two.
- Add the peanuts and stir until they begin to colour& add green chili and saute with the peanuts and cumin for a few more seconds.
- Add the potato and salt, cook for a minute.
- Add the millet, and stir over the heat. Add the water and bring it back to a boil.
- Cover the pan and cook for 15 minutes or until done.
- Add lemon juice. Cover with the lid again and allow to sit for 3 minutes.
- Garnish with coriander and serve hot.

KUTTU KI KHICHDI

Here's another great khichdi to eat during fasts!!

TASTING NOTES

Wholesome grainy khichdi with comforting ghee flavour

SERVES 1	SOAK TIME 6 HRS	COOK TIME 30 MINS

METHOD

½ cup Kuttu whole soaked
¼ cup Moong dal soaked
2 tbsp Fried Peanut
1 big Potato (small cubes)
1 tbsp Chopped Ginger
1 medium Tomato Chopped
1 tsp Whole Cumin Seed
1 Whole Red chili
2 tsp Turmeric
1 tsp Red chili powder
Salt to taste
2 tbsp Ghee
2½ cup water

- Heat ghee in a pan, add cumin seed and red chilli.
- Add potato, fry till light brown ,add tomato, ginger along with all spices and cook till tomato melts.
- Add kuttu and dal. Mix with all the masalas and add hot water. Cook for 15– 20 minutes.
- Cook till it has porridge-like consistency
- Sprinkle fried peanuts and serve hot.

JAEEKI KHICHDI

Jaeeki khichdi made with oats, spinach and dal is the perfect post workout meal!

TASTING NOTES

*Slightly slimy texture cause of oats,
black pepper spices it up*

SERVES 1	SOAK TIME 1 HR	COOK TIME 20 MINS

METHOD

¼ cup moong dal soaked

2 tbsp spinach chopped

2 tbsp oats

1 tsp jeera

2 pieces cinnamon sticks

4-6 pieces whole black pepper

1 piece Kashmiri chilli dry whole

2 tsp ghee

½ tsp red chilli powder

Salt to taste

¾ cup water

- Heat ghee in a pan, add chilli and cook for a minute
- Add jeera, cinnamon, black pepper and stir till fragrant.
- Add spinach and then toss it well till it leaves water.
- Add moong dal and water as for the required consistency.
- Put oats in it and cook well, adding salt as required and then add chilli powder and remove when in proper consistency.
- Serve hot with curd and papad.

MADHUSHREE AND ANINDYA SUNDAR BASU

Food Writers & Photographers
Recipe Chroniclers

TASTING NOTES

Rich ghee flavour,
Ultimate Bengali comfort food

SERVES 4	SOAK TIME 1 HR	COOK TIME 30 MINS

1/2 cup masoor dal
1/4 cup moong dal
1/2 cup Gobindobhog rice
3 large onions or 8-10 whole shallots
2 tbsp chopped garlic
4-5 garlic cloves
1 tsp ginger paste
3 cloves
2 green cardamom
1/2 inch cinnamon stick
1 tsp cumin seeds
1.5 tsp turmeric powder
2 bay leaves
1 tsp sugar
1 cup green peas
2 large potatoes quartered
2 tbsp ghee
1 tbsp mustard oil
2-3 green chilies

METHOD

- Dry roast moong dal over medium flame until the dal becomes just a little bit red. Leave it to cool down.
- Wash and drain the dal, rice, and peas separately.
- In a pressure cooker, add mustard oil, ghee, bay leaves, cinnamon, cardamom, cloves and cumin seeds. Then add the onions, ginger and garlic and fry for a couple of minutes.
- Next, add the potatoes and green peas, and then add the rice and dal mixture. Add turmeric powder, salt and sugar.
- Add 3.5 cups of water and boil. Close the cooker and let it cook for 1 whistle or 10-12 minutes.
- At the same time, boil a liter of water in another pan and keep it hot. Add the boiled water to the khichdi.
- Finally, add ghee and serve hot with some fried fish or begun bhaja, papad or omelette.

THREE BEAN KHICHDI

Our desi dal & bean meets Arborio rice!

TASTING NOTES

Spiced tangy khichdi with garlicky aftertaste

SERVES 2	SOAK TIME 1 HR	COOK TIME 20 MINS

METHOD

1 tbsp oil
3-4 garlic cloves
4-5 cardamom
4-5 peppercorns
2 bayleaf
3 cloves
1 cup Arborio rice soaked
2 tomatoes
2 tbsp Butter beans
2 tbsp broad beans
2 tbsp soya
Coriander to garnish
1 tbsp mixed masala
Red chillies to taste
Salt to taste

- Heat oil, add all the dry spices. Cook well.
- Add tomato, mix it well.
- Add the rice and beans and cover with water.
- Once cooked, season for taste
- Garnish with coriander. Serve hot.

DAL KHICHDI RISOTTO

*You'll be surprised how good
Khichdi with Parmesan & mozzarella tastes!*

TASTING NOTES

*Creamy and cheesy khichdi,
our desi take on traditional moong dal khichdi*

SERVES 2	SOAK TIME 30 MINS	COOK TIME 30 MINS

METHOD

½ cup Boiled toor dal
½ cup Arborio Rice Par cooked
3 tbsp Ghee
1 tsp Mustard Seeds
4-5 Curry leaves
A pinch of Hing
1 big Chopped onion
3-4 Chopped garlic
1 Chopped tomatoes
1 Chopped chilli
1 tsp Turmeric Powder
2 tsp Red chilli powder
1 tsp Roasted Cumin powder
½ cup Stock
¼ cup Mozzarella
2 tbsp Cream
Salt to taste
1 Fried Papad
1 tbsp Parmesan

- Heat ghee in a pan, crackle mustard seeds and curry leaves.
- Add onions, garlic and cook till brown.
- Add the spices and tomatoes, cook till they are soft.
- Once the masala is done, add the cooked dal.
- Then add pre cooked risotto rice, stock water and let it cook for about 5 to 10 minutes.
- Once the rice is cooked al dente, add the parmesan cheese, butter and some cream. Adjust seasoning and finish off by adding in some freshly chopped coriander.
- Garnish with papad chura: crush the papad, ghee and red chili powder. Serve hot.

Glossary of Ingredients

Khichdi - Nutritionally balanced ultimate comfort food.

Rice

1. Basmati rice - Basmati is a variety of long, slender-grained aromatic rice
2. Arborio - an Italian short-grain rice
3. Sona masuri - Sona Masuri is a lightweight and aromatic medium-grain rice
4. Binni rice/Gobindobhog rice - It is a short grain, white, aromatic, sticky rice with a sweet buttery flavor.
5. Black rice - one type of sticky black rice that is indigenous to Manipur.
6. Red rice (Matta) - It is a coarse variety of rice with bold grains and red pericarp.
7. Joha rice - a variety of rice notable for its aroma, delicate and excellent taste.
8. Brown rice - whole grain rice with the inedible outer hull removed.
9. Rice flour - form of flour made from finely milled rice

Dal

1. Moong Dal - Mung beans are called Moong Dal in India. Mung beans, also known as green gram or moong. Both the whole lentils and the split ones with and without skin are used.
2. Lal chana - Also known as kala chana. the chickpea skin is actually brown or reddish brown
3. Toor dal - Yellow split Pigeon peas, also known as Arhar dal
4. Black Urad dal - Urad dal is also known as black Lentils or black gram dal. Use whole or split urad dal which retains the skin and has a strong flavour. Skinned and split urad dal
5. Whole red lentil - Also known as Masoor, it is used in the form of whole, split, with skin and without skin
6. Rajma - Kidney beans
7. Chana dal - Chickpeas
8. Moth dal- Moth beans which is commonly called as mat beans or matki
9. Lobhia- Commonly known as black eyed peas

Spices

1. Namak - Salt
2. Laal Mirch powder - Red chilli powder
3. Haldi - Turmeric
4. Cheeni - Sugar or Granulated sugar
5. Garam masala powder - Blend of different spices
6. Kitchen king - a blend of all major spices, mostly used in north Indian cooking
7. Jeera powder - Cumin powder
8. Dhaniya powder - Coriander powder
9. Gud - Jaggery
10. Sukha Nariyal - Dried coconut

11. Khandeshi garam masala - Maharashtrian masala
12. Methi Dana - Fenugreek seeds
13. Himalayan Pink salt
14. Panch Phoran - a blend of 5 aromatic spices used in Bengali cooking
15. Ghondhorajlebu leaf - a type of lemon grown in bengal
16. Imli Pulp - Tamarind extract
17. Jeera - Cumin
18. Laung - Clove
19. Dalchini - Cinnamon
20. Kali Mirch - Peppercorns
21. Elaichi - Cardamom
22. Kari Patta - Curry leaves
23. Tej Patta - Bay leaf
24. Sabut Dhaniya - Whole dhaniya
25. Sukhi Laal Mirch - Dry red chilli
26. Adrak - Ginger
27. Jeera - cumin
28. Kali Elaichi/Badi Elaichi - Big Cardamom
29. Axone/Akhuni - fermented soya bean of Nagaland, known for its distinctive flavour and smell
30. Hing - Asafoetida
31. Rai - Mustard seeds
32. Stock cube - Veg stock concentrate cube
33. Saunf - Fennel seeds
34. Pudina Powder - Mint leave powder
35. Ajwain - Caraway seeds
36. Boriya chillies - Large round chillies
37. Bird's eye Chilli - Thai green chilli
38. Apple Cider Vinegar- fermented apple juice
39. Dal Makhani Masala - Blend of spices to enhance the taste of dal
40. Tandoori Masala - Combination of coriander, cumin, garlic powder, ginger, cloves, mace, fenugreek, cinnamon, black pepper, cardamom, and nutmeg
41. Saffron - kesar
42. Achaar Masala - Ready pickle masala
43. Pyaaz - Onion
44. Tamatar - Tomato
45. Tamatar Paste - Tomato puree
46. Lasun - Garlic
47. Hari Mirch - Green chillies
48. Aam - Mango
49. Jetun - Olives
50. Til - Sesame

Dry fruits

1. Kaju - Cashews
2. Nariyal - Coconut
3. Kishmish - Raisins
4. Mungfali - Peanuts

Cooking Oils

1. Tel - Vegetable Oil
2. Ghee - Clarified butter
3. Sarson ka tel - Mustard oil
4. Mungfali ka tel - Groundnut oil
5. Makhan - Butter
6. Canola oil
7. Jetun ka tel - Olive oil

Other Ingredients

1. Jaee - Oats
2. Jambu
3. Sabudana - Tapioca
4. Moraiyo - Barnyard Millet
5. Sabut Kuttu - Buckwheat whole grain
6. Ragi vermicelli - Finger millet
7. Gahat - Horse Gram
8. Sooji - Semolina
9. Dalia - broken wheat
10. Godi - Wheat
11. Jau - Barley
12. Chena - Proso Millet

Masala Recipes

Khandeshi Masala Recipe

<u>Ingredients</u>

500gms Dry red chilli
250gm whole Coriander seeds
25gm Bay leaf
25gm Patthar Phool
75gms Khus Khus
75gms Black Pepper
15gm Saunf
15gm Star anise
15gm Javitri
15gm Green Cardamom
15gm Clove

5gm Shahi Jeera
15gm Cinnamon
15gm Black Cardamom
15gm Hing
2 Nutmeg
75gm whole Turmeric

Method

1. Roast everything in a skillet.
2. Cool & grind.

Panch Phoran

Ingredients

2 tablespoons cumin seeds
2 tablespoons nigella seeds (kalonji)
2 tablespoons wild celery seeds (radhuni) or mustard seeds (rai)
2 tablespoons fennel seeds (saunf, mouri)
1 tablespoon fenugreek seeds (methi dana)

Method

1. Mix all the spices in a bowl or directly in a small glass jar.
2. Tightly seal the jar. Store the panch phoron in a cool, dry place.
3. Shake the jar before each use to make sure the spices are evenly distributed.

Book Photography Credits

Tarun Gupta started his career as Digital Lighting Artist and has served the animation films industry for about 3 years. He has some critically acclaimed films credited to him in his portfolio like Delhi Safari and Lootera, and few international projects like Octonauts and Code Lyoko Evolution. Tarun has also worked in Newspaper and Advertising industry with major players like The Times of India and Crayons Advertising. It was during his job in Indonesia when he got interested in photography and after coming back to India he turned his hobby into a profession. Today, he is a photographer by profession, an anchor, a foodie by nature and a producer of many food shows on Youtube. An artist by birth, he likes to do everything with full zeal that makes him stand out.

Location Courtesy : **Aquila Interiors, Jaipur**

Shubham Katrawat is a jaipur based cinematographer/ photographer and mentor who is mainly into films, fashion, advertisement, food and landscape and is been doing the job since 2012. Shubham has been awarded and appreciated by many leading national and international photography communities like bbc uk, natgeo and 35 awards for his unique photography style and work.

Since 1957
Bhagat
MISHTHAN BHANDAR
TM
www.bhagatmishthan.com
info@bhagatmishthan.com
Our Locations
Kishanpole Bazar
Shop no. 185, Kishanpole Bazar, Jaipur
Ph: +91-7821036152
M I Road
M I Road, Opp. Aakashvani, Jaipur
Ph: +91-9001997364
Vaishali Nagar
Bhati Enclave, Main Queens Road, Vaishali Nagar, Jaipur
Ph: +91-7742394202

Healthy isn't always Boring !!

पिंडproduce
earthly pleasures

pindProduce, our flagship Brand for Edible Farm Products, is a sincere attempt at continuing our endeavour of practicing Agriculture and Farming that is spanning over 45 years. In an honest effort to offer pure and natural food products to everyone, we have charted a new path in our jounery - blending conventional practices with modern sensibilities!

Our two generations' experience in chemical-free farming using traditional techniques - has helped us bring out our first offering:

" PindProduce BLACK WHEAT FLOUR"
AN ORGANIC SUPERFOOD!!

Why you should opt for *pind*Produce Black Wheat Flour over Conventional Wheat Flour:

Brought to your homes directly from our farm
Contains Anthocyanin, an antioxidant...
High dietary fibre
Rich in Iron, Zinc and many more vital Nutrients

OUR PRODUCT IS AVAILABLE OFF THE SHELF AT SOME OF JAIPUR'S RENOWNED STORES:

- **SHOPPERS PARADISE**
- **THE COUNTRY STORE**
- **SALTUS CONVENIENCE STORE**
- **TINY ROOTS**

Visit our Website
www.pindproduce.com
+91-8290028226

Follow us on 📷 📘
@pindproduce

You can also savour freshly baked products made from pindProduce Black Wheat Flour at Brot co.

Launching More Products Soon!

www.ingramcontent.com/pod-product-compliance
Lightning Source LLC
Chambersburg PA
CBHW042042110726
48006CB00002B/263